Courage, Revising the Text

Also by William Pitt Root

Song of the Piper
Temperance Poems
Strange Angels: New Poems
Sublime Blue: Selected Early Odes of Pablo Neruda
White Boots: New and Selected Poems of the West
Trace Elements from a Recurring Kingdom: The First Five Books of William Pitt Root
Faultdancing
Invisible Guests
Reasons for Going It on Foot
In the World's Common Grasses
Coot and Other Characters: Poems New & Familiar
Fireclock Four
Striking the Dark Air for Music
The Storm and Other Poems
The Unbroken Diamond: Nightletter to the Mujahadeen

COURAGE

REVISING THE TEXT

POEMS

WILLIAM PITT ROOT

Press 53

Winston-Salem

Press 53, LLC
PO Box 30314
Winston-Salem, NC 27130

First Edition

Cover image, *Man Hanging On in Prague, Czech Republic*,
Copyright © 2006 by William Pitt Root
Used by permision of the artist

About the cover image: First created in 1996, the work known as *Zavěšený muž* (*Hanging Man*) is the vision of Czech sculptor David Černý, whose work can be found all across Prague.

Author photo by Pamela Uschuk
San Francisco Aquarium, 2014

Library of Congress Control Number
2026937925

ISBN 978-1-968783-06-8

I hereby
dedicate
this work
to you,
the readers,
in the spirit
of the nation's original
first lady,
with freedom & justice
for all
&
in the spirit
of
the eternal Coot
who said,
All gold is fool's gold.
If you're so smart,
how come you're rich?

ACKNOWLEDGMENTS

Some of these poems have been published previously in magazines and anthologies whose editors I wish to thank:

THE ATLANTIC: "Wherever" (with different lineation)

COLLEGE ENGLISH: "Listening with the World's Ear"

CREAM CITY REVIEW: "For the Furbearers"

DRUNKENBOAT: "The Unbroken Diamond: Nightletter to the Mujahideen"

KONTINENT (Paris): "The Unbroken Diamond: Nightletter to the Mujahideen" [translated into Russian by Demetri Bobyshev]

MANY MOUNTAINS MOVING: "When Blood Rises to History's Knees"

MEMPHIS REVIEW: "*La Charmeuse des Serpents*"

NEW LETTERS: "*Terribilita*"

NIMROD: "For a Russian Poet Who Has Fallen Silent"

THE OLIVE TREE: "The Snakehandler's Wife"

TELESCOPE: "The Unbroken Diamond: Nightletter to the Mujahideen" (reprinted in *PUSHCART IX*)

Thanks to Mesila Press (Ray Gonzales, editor) which printed "There Is a Permanence That Obliterates the Present" in its broadside series.

Thanks also to Wessel & Leiberman Booksellers and Elliot Bay Book Company (Seattle) which published a broadside of "Courage, Revising the Text."

Thanks also to *New Letters on the Air* which broadcast "*Terribilita*."

And thanks to Raider Eckner of Arcturus Press for publishing "The Unbroken Diamond: Nightletter to the Mujahideen" and to Stewe Claeson for translating it into Swedish.

CONTENTS

MEISTERSINGER

I think of the rooster's armored legs
and eyes crazed wide by sunrise,
and that comb, hot and red,
flopping as he cocks his absurd gaze

and takes into each eye the charge of light
and grips the top rail in his horny grip
as, calling the world to order,
he makes the stars dim and rattle in the sky.

What poet dares with indifference to behold him,
those lyrics edgy as iron, lucid as ice,
that ruthless blood-tongued cry
drawn from a throat sheathed in rainbows of the living flame?

UNDER THE UMBRELLA OF BLOOD

In the shower not ten minutes ago and blind from the vinegar rinse
I was thinking 40. I'm 40
when the stinging reminded me how the Turks used to bet on
just how far a headless man could run—

It was orderly, in its way,
with a band of selected prisoners, troops in attendance, distance markers,
a hammered copper plate fiery red as the sun at the end of a pole:
as the prisoners one at a time ran past the sword took off their heads
and the plate scorched the neck-stumps shut to keep blood pressure up
so the runners ran farther, each stumbling on under the umbrella of blood
until the disfigured collapsed, all legs and loose elbows.

Do you suppose as each head fell staring and revolving
that it could hear the tossed coins clink on the outspread blanket?
Could it see the body running off without it?
As it lay speechless, facing dirt or the sky, as chance would have it,
would it know whether it won or lost for its learned critics?

I wonder, and I rush off to the typewriter wiping my eyes clear,
knowing if I am to get it right
the images under the final downpour must be running
faster than the applauding coins of the world can ever fall.

UNSURPRISED BY HISTORY

If You kill one man it's murder
but if you kill a million it's a statistic.
—Stalin

And just who is this witness so insatiably yawning
this Cyclops whose black socket once
housed a great star's hooded glare
that half-blind Inspector of Good Faith

whose hope is sealed up black in a heart of adamant\
whose twin lungs once inspired blow
immeasurably listless, thin wings flailing
in their blocked breast? His stare is black as patience is

while blood rises to History's knees.
Black as the procession of figures being
stunned into statistics, each a cipher
staggering across pages of unmarked snow.

LISTENING WITH THE WORLD'S EAR

Wind blows the world right.

Dead leaves swirl off
branches tired of them.
Couples leave off midsentence,
turning to watch
curtains flap and tangle.
Dogs cower at doorsteps,
children at their games pause
cocking their heads,
listening with the world's ear.

Tonight air is the river
that washes the earth clean,
dashes against the glass
of windows lit by candles
when the powerlines fail.
No television now
matches this show as
darkness rises in a flood
of leaves and stars
whirling as the walls
tremble and ominously breathe.

Long after the blow is over
tossing sleepers float in dreams
of wind's riverlike rushing,
of homes coming to life.

WHEREVER

you are in the world,
you could no longer
call him a boy,

the one who squats, hovering
like a cloud above
his own reflection

in a rain pooled by
a mound of debris
once his neighborhood

where a hand, not
his own, lies
half closed, as if

beckoning,
half open, as if

letting go.

TERRIBILITA

For Beauty Is Truth, Truth Beauty.
—John Keats

Like curs ravishing trash
for cooked fowl bones
which lure with scent then
rent gut from within,

so we may appear, mouths full
of splintered truths, progressive
facts that defeat us
with our hard victories.

Any song of any stone,
who hears it?
Only the bloodbeat
of the stonedeaf heart

starting and stopping,
starting again. And
those to whom realities sing,
what do we suppose it is

they know that we don't?
Another poet told me once
of a woman abducted
and driven through darkness

to a lake shrouded in fog.
She was raped and hacked
with an axe, thrown
off the dock and left to drown.

When she woke, drowning,
she cried out to the mist
Help, please help me
and out of the mist at last

came a voice, calling
Here, over here
and she swam back
through her own blood

to the dock, gasping
Thank you, thank you
as the axe swung out of the mist
again and again, faceless.

The poet who told me this story
wanted to marry the woman
who lived to tell it to him.
He wanted to know. He wanted to.

THERE IS A PERMANENCE
THAT OBLITERATES THE PRESENT

In that moment required to transfer
lives in a glance,
the light that passes between eyes
has rerouted my life time after time

and I have known
in a manner no court of facts would admit
the fine wrist or steady eye of one
I love in a time parallel to this

or the blue lips of a man
in whose arms I have died
or the broad hands I have killed
or shared bread with on a road

lined with olive trees
as cicadas buzz from the dry shade of stones.
Or I look at a woman and know her
as a father knows the daughter

grieving her lost child,
or as the child has known her,
nuzzling her breast and looking up,
eyes half closed, at her bright chin.

A glance, a tremor in a voice,
the posture a hand assumes
as someone speaks to a stranger,
or simply a human odor

and for an instant this life
is unrecognizable to me
while a code I can neither break nor deny
registers and I respond

with a poem I gaze into later
as into a fire obliterating
the present with its permanence,
hearing as one hears in a shell

the sea suddenly more substantial
than those waves at your ankles
whose foam you may wipe away with that towel
which will never touch the roaring deep within.

THE SNAKEHANDLER'S WIFE

On the hard bleachers of an Arizona gym, she and I
exchange glances and small talk, discovering we've both
worked in Wyoming: She broke horses, I taught poems.
Her husband arranges props on stage as kids mill in
for the assembly. Throughout the performance and display
of coolly docile vipers, and "Freddy" the python draped

across the quaking shoulders of some poor English teacher
speechless while the students squeal, she remains impassive,
bored, I think, at first. Beside her I imagine the countless times
she's seen this act, the myriad faces rapt above the sluggish boa
in gyms from Casper to El Paso, all rigid with the same fear,
and the background of that canned patter as he rattles off

the chilling effects of constriction upon mammals of all sizes.
But no. She's simply been waiting, her lips drawn narrow
as her gaze follows her husband to that basket draped
in a green silk scarf. It starts to quake and even the rat snake
she has let me hold—quick tongue pointing as the dull eyes
stare—
perceptibly stiffens its chill in my hands: The scarf lifts,

slips away. A dark wedge weaves now at the wicker lip,
dips shyly out of sight, rises again as the handler
darts and bobs, a tease to draw it out for us—and out
and out it comes, tall body delicate as wavering black flame
or quivering needle drawn by the attractive force
of his magnetic North. Even as the body arches back,

the head glides counter like a dark laser. He dodges. Her
hands have risen from her lap and hang in air before her
in the powerful attitude of a puppeteer, each encircling
something I finally comprehend. Every movement
of the serpent plays like shadow from those hands, as if
by some remote electric will she could control

each deviation of this force allowing it to turn
and sway until some threat clenches both fists
into radiance, each arm locked stiff to hold it back,
that blunt loaded chamber of the cobra's head,
until her husband, unsuspecting, drops
the quenching silk upon it, bows for his applause.

COLD FRONT

All across those neighborhoods milky blue below,
lights melt through the frost-blind windows
forced down tight against their jambs, as if
this chill were so easily excluded from
the rooms huddled in such homes.

And from the hill sloping to that valley
filling up with heat and light from rivers
hundreds of miles off, where salmon each fall
run in from the ocean like memories fresh
from a prehistoric past,

I turn in the front seat to look up through
the frost-charged glitter of this air that flows
in its silent flood down from the Arctic
interrupted here by these spectral peaks,
look through it to the stars that are not burning

yet seem to burn, seem to consume themselves
in such a constant fury of radiance that I,
billions of miles away, am momentarily aware
just how brief these sorrows are we cling to,
how frail these hopes evolving out of agony,

wounds a twinkle heals in lives the next blink
can extinguish. If only we knew how rare
in such a universe this sufferance is— rarer
than live orchids in the void, more precious, almost,
than forgiveness working its way back through the dark.

IN THE HOUSE OF DENIAL

No fear here say the Chattering Teeth
no cruelty here the Thin Lips
nothing but love the Shrill Mother's Bruises
Nothing but love that's better than nothing

No fear here waves the Clenched Fist
no cruelty the Augers of Twisting Light
nothing but love the Heap of Staring Ashes
Nothing but love that's better than nothing

No fear here cry the Knotted Fingers
no cruelty the Eyes Averted
nothing but love the Limping Child
Nothing but love that's better than nothing

No fear here stutters the Split-lipped
no cruelty the Hands That Won't Stop Serving
nothing but love the Bulimic Daughter
Nothing if not love the feast of love

REMEMBERING THE SEA-ELEPHANT

Perhaps it is time for Candor,
with its big beak and clubbed feet,
to start its dance of extinction
toward the Smithsonian. Now

while a few living members
of its race are still abroad
—the Gaffe, the Blunder, the Booboo,
the Inoperative Statement,

the Unauthorized Leak,
the Regrettable Figure of Speech.
Now, while we still can tell one
when we meet it out and about.

Remember the Sea-Elephant
at the turn of the past century,
how only nine could be found
by the Smithsonian expedition

which stuffed seven for us. Oh,
two were let go, perhaps because
the crew was weary or orders simply
read *Remember the Ark.* That pair

coupled relentlessly, for company.
Now how they flourish at the edge
of our continent! So let us
send out our crew to snare Candor

for the permanent archives, leaving
a couple of Unguarded Remarks
at large, to do what they've
always done at the edge

of the continent of Lies
and Diplomacy— frisking openly,
enjoying the rocking waters,
nurturing the oddness

of their miraculous persistence,
preserving it for those of us
who may happen eventually
to that coast where we wonder

at the mewing and roaring,
the grumbling and cooing
in ourselves echoing
out there, loud and sure,

where prudent stone
is milled by careless surf
into the stuff we stand on
if we are to stand.

AT HAZARD

1.

Because there is a crisis overseas
we gather in this well-lit hall
proud with banners,
loud with poems.

In rooms where they meet
there's little light,
less security,
and it's dangerous
even to hint
at the danger. So remote
from our lives
are theirs— and so hazardous—,
that even poetry is taken seriously. Taken away.

2.

We come for the spasmodic eloquence
of grainy smuggled filmstrips—
jostled heads and shoulders,
clubs coming down, gritty darkness—,
come because we need to see
such images projected through
the elemental absence in ourselves,
the loneliness their courage
touches, haunts. We are familiar
with the on-going history
of bloated bodies heaped
less carefully than cordwood
in city dumps on our own continent—
peasants with their thumbs wired
swollen black behind them,
women whose suffering defies race

slumped against adobe walls,
dark shawls drawn up to their brimming gaze.
Increasingly this vision taxes us
with what we mistake for our own
helplessness; we turn from it now
to these women stark against banked snow,
the men beside them bulky
in those ill-fitted suits tailored
to standards we find oddly familiar
and endearing on grandfathers we've seen
like that in snapshots, young.

3.

In this most recent crisis
the crowds we watch stand back
from the banked flowers of
crude memorials in snow, as if
these flowers were flames too
contagious to approach. Still
they do gather, opening their hands
as they must, to warm them,
the ranked statues frozen behind them—
tanks and troops one word thaws.
But what light won't cast
shadows? Where courage
has assembled, risks attend.
Not only the dramatic danger
of wild shots deflected
in a cheering plaza,
not the clack of nightsticks
clattering through nightmare;
not this order of danger

but the ordinary error
of gratefully heaping upon
the marked shoulders of another
those burdens which are ours.
                                        If,
unwittingly, we keep our heroes
at a distance, even admiration
must evolve subtle betrayals.
The crosshairs of History
can only martyr those
whose courage we refuse
to accept in ourselves.

4.

The llamas of Peru are wise
and curiously just: overburden one
and all lie down, unbudging,
until the shifted loads
are made bearable for each. This
protest is a start
we honor best
by reaching into the fire
for an acetylene flower— courage
ignited in others by specific need
taken up by us
as a condition of bloodhood.

          So it is
we begin, if
we begin: awkward
but moved, uncertain
but moved. Moved

half-willingly
beyond ourselves, thrust
past the tremulous periphery
of everything familiar
and out into darkness again
where a thousand local injustices
burn, oblivious and constant
as appointed stars.

5.

Until that hour with its new stance arrives
geared to risk, we here are at hazard
of attending a diversion,
a natural history of shadows,
our most passionate applause the sound of two hands
clapping in a dream, shadow on shadow,
in a place we haven't dared claim for our own.

Here, we are learning to take strength
from others already
honoring that charge
lodged so deeply in our lives
that we must wholly re-imagine ourselves
if those destroyed in one place are anywhere to survive.

FOR THE FURBEARERS OF 5TH AVENUE

Bright colors attract predators no less
than they attract sexual partners.
—Richard Dawkins (Cambridge Zoologist)

When through the golden fur
your body ripples gliding
over asphalt and concrete
in the same sun and moon

that leopard you wear
once knew at the base
of Kilimanjaro (towering
over plains he would prowl

patiently following striped herds
for the old and young
whose helplessness
beckoned his hunger

and answered his jaws with blood
as simply as the sun shines down
to heat March buds
or your skin stretching

tanned and oiled
on the expensive sands
your adoring mate pays for),
when I see you on the street

gracefully exact in charms
worn lightly as your youth,
I succumb to that attraction
your whim has assumed

pulling this coat from the rack,
that zoo of loveliness and death
run by the acquired powers
you take for granted now.

But later, when I think of you
strolling without awareness
of the naked spectral beast
your tastes provoked

into a hunter's cage
10,000 miles away
below the same sky
we're still breathing,

what I see is this:
The ingenious contraption
in which the leopard's skills
at outrage and rending

are so tightly confined
he cannot turn to tear
with those clawed feet
the bars that hold him.

Cannot protest the hand
that lifts his tail
as he stands incredulous
while the steel rod glowing red

is shoved into his anus
which seizes like a fist
around the blade a mugger
in a nightmare slowly

presses through your heart,
removing, as you fall wide-eyed
to the familiar pavement,
that garment you once assumed

desire could possess.
The skinner starts to work
soon as the writhing stops,
inserts the sharp tip

into the charred ass
and delicately moves
toward the throat still locked
around the last rising scream.

Yes, you are beautiful
and the colors wind explores
lifting that fur,
lofting your own brilliant hair,

dazzle as they are intended to.
Oh, careless creature,
innocent of any thoughts
of outraged agony,

I fear for you. Such beauty
as our world provides
is so quickly discovered.
And you have made yourself attractive.

LA CHARMEUSE DES SERPENTS

After Henri Rousseau

And who will not hear the flute
  toward whom the serpent tends
    out into vacant air

away from its lush jungle
  of moongreen leaves
    and the long darkness of the heart?

Her black hair flows
  and falls from her black skull
    across black shoulders,

her lunar eyes spirits
  in the night of her face.
    Her muscles, undulant and firm,

ride the moonlight
  of her bones like snakes
    that writhe around a glowing branch.

There is no age
  whose grasses have not risen
    to her possession, whose waters

have not calmed
  when the moon came down
    to know her thrilling song.

Nor is there any song,
  any serpent, moon, or woman—
    except in our need to know them,

know them all.

FOR A RUSSIAN POET
WHO HAS FALLEN SILENT

I am going away, going away
Into the bright, distant steppes,
Where rushing dogs follow that taut
Track, woven into chain.
. . .
I'm going away. What do I care
How you live without me?
—Yunna Moritz

Every kind of silence intervenes—
You vanish into awful brilliance, dreaming
that your blouse becomes a veil of snow
across your back there below polar sky
where a blizzard's almost human voice
resounds, where the elements are complicated
by your urgent imagination of one man, the first
to enter this frozen zone of your winter,
and by one woman, yourself, a witness
to that lone figure. You study him, wondering
"Why is he here so soon? What has he
come to escape, or look for?" Knowing
that where the land is ice, heart must provide,
in your dream of courage you coax him
to regard the earth whose icy skyward
stare is blank as Sleeping Beauty's
and to feel stirring within him
that deep kiss, the antidote. . . .

Halfway round the earth,
after reading you the first time,
at midnight, restless in a valley
where fall trees toss in moonlight
rustling like skirts stiffened by chill,
I watch an arctic wind inscribe
the glass with frost, my live breath stunned
into blinding crystals. It will be
a hard winter. We will need each other.

But they say you are seldom heard now
in your homeland. Whatever the apple is
lodged invisibly in your throat,
out of gratitude and need
I send with my greeting
this kiss: Use it
to reopen
the proud circle
      of your frozen lips,
spiritual breathing hole
at which that Northern hunter,
kneeling, may still hope, if
he is patient and attentive,
to be sustained.

TYRANNY AND ART

After Kierkegaard and You Know Who

Because he has spoken freely in the land of a tyrant,
because he has offered a King,
royal smiths are fashioning this huge brazen bull for him,
crafted ingeniously to contain on the beaten floor of its belly,
above that gradual fire the King's own hand shall set,
this one man, naked, crouching.

A hollow
instrumental to the man's breathing
shall wind through the monstrous throat
where it must further serve to flute
the bitter cries of his long burning
through lengths of gold and silver
so subtly turned, so torturously tuned
that of such cries
is made the sweetest music.

Strip him.
Give him to the Bull. The king tonight
is restless and would warm his hands
at the fire and by the conversions
of an enemy be soothed.

KOSOVO

She's been wandering for days. Nights at her age must be long. With only snow and the moon. How she lost her family no one knows. Whether in battle or by execution. They lay in the courtyard welded to earth by surprised blood frozen too hard even for the curs. Now she wanders snowy roads. With strangers. They once were her husband and sons. How much does she suffer? Her shoes are low-cut, the snow is ankle-deep. You can see how the melted snow has frozen into her blue socks. How the cold leather is wet and stiff. These are kinds of things you can know.

She is sitting beside the rutted dirt road staring at mountains black as headlines on a page she cannot turn.

THE ARGUMENT
or How Political Poems Still Figure

Who was it that said the contemporary artist risks self-mutilation
because it's the nature of modern pain
to drive us inward rather than outward? We are

he said—it was Pasternak—like powerful locomotives
with their headlamps affixed backwards
racing over rails unseen through darkness unacknowledged.

THE UNBROKEN DIAMOND:
Nightletter to the Mujahideen

1.

Yes, your stories reach us
just as the grit once a summit in our country
reaches you, imperceptibly
dusting your upturned faces
                    calling on Allah,
scanning the indifferent blue skies
            armed with helicopters—
that iron nightmare politics has built
into your lives.

Our sunsets
intensified by that volcanic ash
remind us
of your tragedy, your sunsets
behind villages
            in flames
from the bombings
where figures stumbling darkly up from rubble
search out
the others who do not rise.

Stories of
the unbroken diamond of your resistance.

2.

Here
those nine
spring days are called
"The Childrens Revolt"—

as if
your children could be children, as if
the girl fifteen who tore her veil off
          and handed it
to a soldier *Here, give me your rifle*
could any longer be a child

anywhere.

3.

Or as if
at the head of the column of chanting students,
Nahid Saed, first
of the seventy to die that day—
thirty
rounds point blank in her body—, as if
that daughter
who became the daughter of your land
could turn
her ruined face
to answer a father again.

4.

The stories reach us—

how you refuse
to attend an unveiling,
turning away
from a new flag whose bright face is
the old lie of complicity,
and how
troops fire into your faces,
Afghan troops
inexplicably your own.

Their faces freckle with your blood.

5.

Yes, we do hear
how you stone the limousine
of the Soviet ambassador
until again
foreign guns in the hands of your countrymen
respond,
able to kill you,
unable
to stop your carrying of the dead and shattered into a high school
while 5,000 students, male and female,
answer on the occupied streets of Kabul
crying
Death to Babrak Karmal!
Death to Bresnev!
Where is America?
Are we not human beings?

6.

We hear of that ten-minute slaughter
of students
by machine-gun fire, hear then
the charge of 2,000 horsemen—
swords drawn, electric cattle-prods high,
the ancient weapons and the new—
into the huddled dead and dying,
the screams of horses, and your cries.

                                        Finally
there is the low moaning,
arms lifting like fronds,
the thud of retreating hooves
muffled by earth trodden to red mud.

And we hear of your four more days of resistance.

7.

We hear
how when the armored unit
surrounding you
blazes, you answer
simply with your blood until 2,000 more
rise up,
grab one soldier,
stab out his eyes—
as if to kill him were too simple,
as is to blind him were to eradicate what he has seen.

8.

And we hear
of the puppet show that night
when televised officials
deny
those bodies
in whose wet flames of blood
your hands
burn and burn
until even the blinded soldier must see by their light.

9.

Yes, all these stories reach us
in blocks of black-and-white in those columns
we would hurl back

embowered by every mile and lie
between us
to scourge your nation clean.

If wishes were pumice.

If words were scouring stones.

10.

But all that reaches you
from us
is apolitical ash, proof
of an old magnificence
shocked to dust—
grit as hard
and fine
as the skin
of a pearl run across the tooth
of a mujahidan skillfully determining
its true worth.
He spits
as he continues to watch
the hammered blue sky and chants
to himself
ancient songs from a village turned
in 90 seconds
to light and the
smoldering limbs of family and friends,
the songs of shepherds
accustomed to solitude
now being used to keep armed men
aware of each other in the high passes.

11.

Those wornwood crooks
you've managed your flocks with
cleverly tend
new herds now:
                                        Soviet iron-tracks
your scouts lure
through ravines you seal with boulders
pried loose
by those shepherd's staffs.

Trapped and terrified
too late,
they spatter
canon and machine-gun fire
against the indestructible cliffs
where you are hidden, waiting
for the exhausted silence
you will break with dusty grins
and a calculated avalanche of native stone.

12.

Only once
have I stood on a summit
high as those passes
you guard like wives—
ten years ago,
while some of you were still children
playing among the billowing tents
at the hoop-and-shadow games,
too shy
even to glance at those with whom
your children
have been born and raised.

We'd driven east
through the thinning darkness
those three friends and I,
toward dawn and the mountain
we climbed all morning long.
Climbing
we looked back
at a world all wilderness,
not unlike our own, and at the laketops,
each a remote
mirror to a bright fragment
of that vastness
no one sees all at once. Then
I began to comprehend
the Indian comparison of
climbing the mountain
to knowing God, ridge
after ridge beckoning, each
a false summit,
until
only the euphoria

of feeling the mountain rise
to meet each step
kept us going— past excitement
and laughter, weariness
and silence,
past each new sense of limit
we imagined to be our last,
beyond pumice
            to rockface,
into snow and ice
where the mountain disappeared
below us, leaving
us suspended
high on the rim of wildfire and ice,
able to witness the world as a ring
to which our connection
had vanished.

13.

This is the mountain,
Fire Mountain,
whose summit circles the earth,
invisible to the eye where you are
except as a tint at sunset,
grit between your teeth
and the teeth of your wives and sons and daughters,
the teeth of your enemies—
this trace of Godhead inconspicuously everywhere.

14.

Miraculously, overnight
the countryside—
so long a familiar nightmare
where crops are burned routinely
so only the stones mature—
is wonderfully ablaze,
littered with glittering firetrucks,
          ballons, sticks of chewing gum
and, most irresistible of all,
little dolls that smile.

And every item ingeniously
detects
even the lightest touch:
                              Ffffooooffff
and magically the hand
disappears, the fingers
are suddenly stubble
charred as the fields, and their scalps
shed braids of ragged blood and dust,
naked as all the mountain meadows
              goats have overgrazed.

Ffffooooffff and wonder takes the shape of fire
formerly a child
     scrambling and billowing
in the grass,
clawing now
at eyes too intently innocent
          to suspect the gift
                              come from nowhere.

15.

Wouldn't workers somewhere wonder
why they've been devising toys
that blast, stun, blind
            then inextinguishably burn
so the last thing some child's eyes
ever will behold are
            her own hands
curling into claws?

                        How
can human hearts so crudely hardened
contrive nonetheless with a delicacy so meticulous?

16.

I am a man whose one power is telling.
I tell you this:
                I would give you words
massive as boulders to roll against tanks and iron-tracks,
delicate words to heal the roses driven
by dum-dum shells into your flesh,
words of silk and gut to restore each maimed limb
from the truckload of arms and legs
        hacked off in a single village
and dumped in a square in Kabul,
words to re-root tongues
torn from the mouths
of those who warned you,
milk-words rich and white for the myriad infants
held to the shrunken breasts of mothers
starving in Kohat and dozens of camps
thousands flee to over Parachinar Pass
through the Speen Ghar Mountains.

17.

—I would give you
wind-words to dispel the experimental gasses
of Soviet advisors,
to disperse the yellow rain and scatter
mists of blue and green
dust,
each composed
to destroy in another way
the frail machinery of the human body,
hearts and minds betrayed by their own blood.

18.

—I would give you
healing words to mend the lungs and shorted nerves
and bursting veins
of the hundreds, the thousands
of you who fall gasping
and hacking up sudden blood
with your nose-blood gagging you
and ear-blood hot along your necks,
anus-blood and manroot-blood scalding your legs
        to your boots and bare feet,
eye-blood blinding you as you look up
to take aim.

19.

—I would give you
Heat-seeking words to bring down the observers taking
notes in helicopters circling overhead
timing
on stop-watches
with Cyrillic numerals
how long it takes before
you with your muzzle-loaders
and your women and children with slingshots and rocks
collapse, then
how much longer it takes you to stop writhing altogether
on sodden ground among the unscathed huts.

20.

Lastly
I would draw
          from Nahid Saed
the thirty traitorous pieces of lead
and give them to her
for charms. To the eyes
of your women
raped like the land, helplessly shamed
by the violence of men
whose shadows dark as vultures
seed the valley with fire and char,
I would restore
the brilliance and tenderness
toward you,
toward themselves. Toward your children.

If words were scouring stones.

If wishes were pumice.

21.

With the stone of helplessness
huge under my tongue,
I tell you your story is heard.

Your story is being heard.

COURAGE, REVISING THE TEXT

Time was, it wasn't uncommon for us kids to be taught that
courage was right and clean, reliable as daylight. Maybe
it wore a cape no shame could stain, maybe it
faced danger with a bulletproof grin or
wielded a bigger gun than the other guys,
eyes clear as the thoughtless sky.
                                        And only losers
hunched in ash heaps smoldering and rank,
fingering the octaves of their losses
in tatters of regret at twilight.

And so by the time we'd sprouted beards or breasts
and, at an hour not on our childhood clocks,
nuzzled the one with the other a time or two,
we knew ourselves for the cowards we were becoming,
and geared for a long haul cobbled with the boulders
of loss and pebbles of minor compensation,
no longer searching our mirrors for heroes.
But years require revision in the heart's first text
now don't they, so we recast the characters and plot
not as we imagined them but as they've come to be.
Just now I think of Smilovic, the Croat cellist,
refugee among refugees in a cave above Sarajevo,
bumming smokes and brandy shamelessly all afternoon
from his NPR interviewer, and how, at twilight,
seated among dozens of strangers
he shifts, taking up his bow to perform
in that darkness which is history and fear,
how his sweetly drawn music manifests an order
resonant with beauty, yes, but nuanced, too,
with memories barbed by hope and all the anguish
of an audience geared hard by survival now,
scarred by murder, rape, and the forced witness
of degradation no heart withstands unbroken.

As I listen I am hushed by hard news
of this one's fate, by the image of him
sitting on the heaped ashes of a library
playing at first alone and for himself
so that the enemy would know the spirit
of a people lives, and is not silenced
—not by flame, bomb, bullet, or
brutality that seems to know no end;
alone he sat there calling forth
music and the crowd that gathered
listened as he played until at last
they sang, giving ashen silence a new name
that cannot be translated without flame.

William Pitt Root is at home wandering the San Juan and Weminuche Wilderness with his wolf dog Mojo Buffalo Buddy. His first fifteen poetry collections reflect a life active both within and without academia teaching, first at Slippery Rock University, then as far from academia as it gets—in a factory outside of Stockton, California, as bouncer in the Sweet Chariot Bar in Seattle, in a copper mine, and in the bilge of an oil tanker. He has taught as a Poet-In-Schools to children on five Native nations as well as in public schools in southern states. For twenty years, Bill taught creative writing and Native American Literature at Hunter College in Manhattan. From 1995-2002 he served as first Poet Laureate of Tucson, Arizona. His work appears in *The NYer*, *Atlantic*, *Poetry*, *Ploughshares* and in other journals and anthologies. Recipient of fellowships from Guggenheim and Rockefeller Foundations, NEA, Stanford University and US/UK Exchange Artists Program, Root's recent books are *Strange Angels* and *Sublime Blue, Translations of the Odes of Pablo Neruda*. He is a poetry editor at *Cutthroat, a Journal of the Arts*. He divides his time between Bayfield, Colorado, and Tucson, Arizona, where he lives with his wife, the better poet, Pam Uschuk.

www.ingramcontent.com/pod-product-compliance
Lightning Source LLC
LaVergne TN
LVHW051020080826
845145LV00009B/2726

* 9 7 8 1 9 6 8 7 8 3 0 6 8 *